Them and Us

Five plays adapted from
television scripts to
read and discuss

Roger Parkes

Edward Arnold

© Roger Parkes 1985

First published in Great Britain 1985 by
Edward Arnold (Publishers) Ltd, 41 Bedford Square, London WC1B 3DQ

Edward Arnold (Australia) Pty Ltd, 80 Waverley Road, Caulfield East,
Victoria 3145, Australia

British Library Cataloguing in Publication Data

Parkes, Roger
Them and us: five plays adapted from television
to read and discuss.
I. Title
822'.914   PR6066.A6953

ISBN 0-7131-8286-5

Text set in 11/14 Rockwell
by The Castlefield Press, Moulton, Northampton
Printed and bound by Whitstable Litho Ltd.

Contents

Introduction

Many of the problems facing young people can lead them to end up in the juvenile court. The magistrates may not have the solutions; but that doesn't diminish the drama, either of the courtroom confrontation itself or of the events leading up to it.

Them and Us originated from the Central Television play series first transmitted in the autumn of 1985. In revising the television scripts for use in the classroom, I have been able both to elaborate on the background causes of the offence and to streamline the trial process – while also enhancing the overall pace and character development.

Besides the drama of the plays themselves, it is intended that pupils should benefit from the insights they offer into their everyday problems. To this end, each play concludes with a range of questions under the headings of *Understanding the action*, *Making up your mind*, *Ideas for writing*, and *Drama work*.

R.P.

Neighbours

Janie Smith, 16, left school early and has mothered the family ever since her mum left home a year ago.

Len Smith, and his brother **Peter**, 13, are a scrappy, prickly couple of scamps.

Jack Smith, their dad, is without a job, a wife, luck or self-confidence.

Patrick Ryan, 15, and his sister, **Kate**, 14, are both fiercely loyal to their family and its Irish origins. Both have Irish accents.

Seamus Ryan, 12, is a DIY lad, a chicken keeper and a rebel.

Sheena and **Michael Ryan** are 10 and 11 and always speak at the same time.

Mrs May Ryan is upright and honest, and is overwhelmed by her eight children.

Mr John Ryan, although he respects his wife's religion, is less tolerant than her.

The magistrate is a man who finds the case of the two neighbouring families funny.

The prosecuting lawyer is a woman who doesn't find it at all funny. Also: **Court clerk**.

*Five **Ryan** children are in court along with their parents. Also present are the **Smith** family from next door – three children and their dad. Fade into court.*

Prosecutor   Your worships, it seems that a row broke out across the garden fence. Tempers flared into violence and then a running battle which ended up in a brawl in the street. This might very well have lead to severe injury but for the arrival of a policeman . . .

Fade to later after the policeman's evidence.

Clerk	Well, children, what have you got to say? (*pause*) All eight of you denying these serious charges. What happened? (*pause*)
Janie	(*abrupt*) It was those eggs started it.
Seamus	(*shrill*) Your fault for nicking them!
Len	(*angry*) Poisoners!
Patrick	Thieves!
Clerk	Quiet now!
Kate	Goes back long before that.
Janie	(*bitter*) And who's fault's that, 'Catty' Ryan?!
Clerk	*Quiet.* This isn't a classroom. (*pause*) Kate Ryan, you go into the witness box first. Take the Bible in your right hand and read the card.
Kate	I promise before Almighty God, that the evidence I shall give shall be the truth, the whole truth and nothing but the truth.
Clerk	You said the trouble goes way back?
Kate	Months. Ever since they moved in last year.
Janie	(*abrupt*) You started it!
Clerk	Quiet, Jane. Let Kate speak first, then you can have your say. (*pause*) Well, Kate?
Kate	Far as I'm concerned it was their filthy fires started it.
Magistrate	Fires?
Kate	Bonfires, sir, lit sure as daylight every washing-day.

Fade back a month or so to actual row over washing in the Ryan's garden.

Kate	(*furious*) O no! Dirty pigs! Mum, will you come and see . . .
Janie	(*mocking*) 'Mummy, mummy . . .'
Kate	*Ah* – I thought you'd be hiding somewhere abouts.
Janie	Wasn't hiding!
Kate	So just why must you choose now to light up?
Janie	There's no law says I can't.

Kate	Dirty great smuts all over these nappies.
Janie	(*mocking*) Oh – what a shame . . .
Kate	(*angry*) All that black smoke – you're burning engine oil again, aren't you!
Janie	I really wouldn't know what's on there.
Kate	(*indignant*) Of course you do! Deliberate – just the instant we get a load of washing pegged out!
Janie	Too bad . . .
Kate	You could have waited!
Janie	(*sharp*) Wait forever then, wouldn't I. Everyday's washing-day with a family of ten! Catholic rabble!
Kate	How's that?
Janie	You heard me, peasant.
Kate	(*sharp*) At least we're a *proper* family – instead of a load of motherless scroungers!

Fade to later, the boys now facing each other across the garden fence.

Len	(*angry*) You lot calling us scroungers, are you?
Patrick	(*sharp*) Too right! It's as much as your dad can do to get himself down the dole queue, much less fix up that tip you live in.
Pete	(*angry*) Rubbish!
Seamus	(*laughing*) That's right – rubbish tip!
Len	I'll have you, Seamus!
Patrick	(*sharp*) And we'll have the council on you!
Len	You what?
Patrick	Stink, flies, weeds – all those oily bonfires . . .
Pete	(*giggles*) Just sending up smoke signals, ain't we.
Seamus	What?
Pete	Signalling the Paras to come after you IRA scum.
Len	(*laughing*) Need the pest officers not the Paras.
Seamus	Scabs!
Pete	Paddy tinkers!
Seamus	Scroungers!
Patrick	Leave 'em, Seamus. They're not worth a yell.
Seamus	But . . .

Patrick	Come on away.
Len	Cowards!
Pete	Yellow spuddies!
Len	Guttless wonders!

Fade to **Ryan** *family tea.*

Patrick	(*angry*) Cowards, it is now!
Mrs Ryan	Just ignore them, Patrick.
Patrick	An insult like that?
Kate	Never!
Mrs Ryan	We can, Katie-girl, and we will.
Kate	But, mum . . .
Mrs Ryan	(*persisting*) Violence wasn't ever God's way, nor shall it be ours.
Patrick	All the things they're saying about us at school. . . .
Mrs Ryan	(*interrupting*) Prayers, Patrick Ryan, not curses. Isn't that so, John?
Mr Ryan	Your mother's right, lad. Pray that the poor devil will find himself a job and some self-respect along with it. That's the surest thing'll heal their troubles.
Kate	(*sharp*) Won't stop them ruining the washing.
Seamus	Or nicking our eggs!
Mrs Ryan	Tolerance, Seamus. Turn the other cheek.
Patrick	(*laughing*) They'll nick that and all if he does!

Fade to **Smith** *family tea.*

Pete	IRA whimps.
Mr Smith	Shut up and eat your egg.
Pete	It tastes funny.
Len	(*giggles*) Came from a funny place.
Janie	(*laughing*) Yes! An Irish place and all!
Pete	(*in mock horror*) Ugh!!
Len	What do you call an Irishman with half a brain?
Pete	*Gifted!*
Mr Smith	(*disapproving*) Them jokes can get very boring.
Len	(*laughing*) It's not a joke – it's a fact!
Pete	Yes! Specially them whimpy Ryans!

4

Mr Smith	Knock it off, you two.
Janie	They're the narks who've been snooping on you, dad – telling on you down the DHSS.
Mr Smith	No proof it's them.
Janie	Look how they're always calling us parasites, calling this place a tip and that.
Len	Dumb lot of Holy Joes . . .
Pete	IRA whimps . . .
Mr Smith	Will you stop saying that!
Janie	Well I don't like being called a motherless scrounger, least of all by that Catty Ryan.
Len	Or by Patrick. . . .
Pete	Or that Seamus . . .
Janie	Just cos mum went off and you can't find yourself no work . . .
Mr Smith	(*hassled*) Look, will you lot just leave it out, eh!
Janie	But, dad, if they're into snooping and sneaking on you . . .
Mr Smith	We don't *know* it's them . . .
Pete	But, dad . . .
Mr Smith	Shut up, Pete, and eat your egg!

Fade to later in garden.

Seamus	Hey, scum, what you got there?
Pete	What?
Seamus	Behind your back.
Pete	Nothing.
Seamus	Show us then.
Pete	Why should I?
Seamus	Thief . . . .
Pete	I'm *not!*
Seamus	Then prove it. Show us.
Pete	(*casual*) Just an old hen's egg, that's all.
Seamus	Knew it! *Thief.* Hey, mum . . . .
Pete	What you blowing about? It ain't stolen . . .
Seamus	'Course it is!
Pete	It was on *our* side of the fence.
Seamus	Liar . . .

Pete (*laughing*) If your dumb hens can't tell which side's which . . . .

Seamus 'Course they can! Give it here . . . .

Pete *No.* Finder's keepers!

Seamus Thief! Hey, come back here! Where you going?

Pete Have me tea. (*laughs*) Egg butty.

Seamus (*calling after him*) I hope it makes you spew! Weazel!

Fade to the **Ryan** *boys' bedroom. Kate is knocking on the locked door to be let in.*

Kate (*calling*) Seamus, you monkey, what are you up to in there?

Seamus Go away.

Kate (*calling*) Open this door or I'll tell mum. (*pause*) Come on! (*Pause as* **Seamus** *lets her into the bedroom.*)

Seamus Promise you won't tell.

Kate Depends what you're up to. (*She starts to laugh as she sees what he's up to.*) Hey, into secret cooking, are you.

Seamus (*excited*) Not for meself, Katie. For that scum next door.

Kate (*laughing*) Well, if it's dung cakes you're going to cook 'em, there's no sense using good eggs like those.

Seamus (*giggles*) They're just shells, look.

Kate How's that?

Seamus See how I drilled these wee holes in each end and then blew out the insides for our tea.

Kate Okay, Merlin, so what's in the other bowl?

Seamus Take a sniff.

Kate (*horrified after sniffing it*) Holy Mother, what you got mixed up in there?

Seamus (*gleeful*) Mustard to make it yellow, castor oil for speed, shampoo to clean out their mouths . . .

Kate (*delighted*) You wee devil you!

Seamus	Here, just hold the funnel so I can pour it into the shells.
Kate	(*holding funnel*) How'll you plug up the holes?
Seamus	Putty – then smear some hen's poopsy over to hide the plugs. Then stick 'em in that nest under the hedge.
Kate	You're a holy terror, Seamus!
Seamus	Dad was telling me it's how they used to poison the vermin on the farm.
Kate	Oh aye? Smith vermin, eh!

Fade to **Smith** *kitchen the next morning.*

Janie	Be late for school if he ain't in soon.
Len	It's okay – here he comes. (*Peter enters triumphantly clutching four eggs.*)
Pete	Turrah!
Janie	How many?
Pete	*Four!*
Len	Brill . . . .
Pete	Breakfast special!
Janie	(*laughing*) Hurry it up, then. Len, get the pan heating. Pete, crack them into that bowl while I get the mixer . . . .
Mr Smith	(*disapproving*) I've told you lot before about nicking . . .
Pete	On *our* side, dad – that nest under the hedge.
Mr Smith	(*firm*) It's still nicking!
Janie	Here, stick in those left-over spuds from last night.
Pete	Okay.
	Pause as the first omelette is cooked.
Janie	Here you are then – half each. Hurry it down . . . .
Pete	(*chewing*) Tastes funny . . .
Len	(*the old joke*) Came from a funny place! (*He, too, chews then spits it out in disgust.*) Ugh!
Janie	What's wrong?
Len	It's *vile!*
Pete	I'm going to pewk!

Janie	Not in here, you ain't!
Len	Me first!
Pete	*No....*
	The two rush out for the toilet leaving Janie and her father in alarm.
Mr Smith	Here, let's smell that food.
Janie	Awful!
Mr Smith	(*sniffing the omelette*) I recognise that smell.
Janie	One of the eggs must have been bad....
Mr Smith	Not bad, love. Doctored. Look here at this shell.
Janie	Hey! Those crafty, rotten Paddies!

Fade to later that day after school.

Len	How many bags you got ready, Janie?
Jane	Dozen or so.
Pete	Bags for what?
Len	Soot bombs.
Pete	Great!
Janie	(*gleeful*) We'll give that 'Catty' some washing for her line!
Pete	I could get some old dung down the riding stables.
Len	Brill!
Janie	And there's this bucket of slops.
Len	Pooh!
Janie	If we could sort of balance it up on their shed then somehow tug it down over them....
Pete	*Splurch!*
Len	You mean, like an ambush? Plop with the slops then start flinging the bags and dung and that?
Pete	Pow-Pow-POW!
Janie	So how do we lure them?
Len	Eh?
Janie	They won't come out if they know we're waiting.
Pete	Easy to get Seamus out.
Len	How?
Pete	Toss a banger in the hen run and set his old hens going.

Fade to juvenile court as at start. **Seamus** *is now in the witness box.*

Seamus We're all at our tea when there's this blooming almighty *bang* from down the hen run. Fowls all going bonkers, dog yapping . . . Then, when we all dashed out to see what's what, they're hiding in waiting to start flinging all this muck at us . . . (*The* **Smiths** *start sniggering and jeering.*)

Pete Pow, POW!

Clerk Be quiet.

Prosecutor So what did you do, Seamus?

Seamus Well we went after them – heads down, over the fence and at 'em. Of course they all ran for it. (*Jeers in denial from the* **Smiths**.)

Prosecutor And then?

Seamus Well, we managed to catch them on the green out the front and started to sort them out.

Prosecutor And it was then that the policeman arrived?

Seamus Yes – and just as well for them he did.

Prosecutor What do you mean by that?

Seamus Someone could have got hurt.

Prosecutor Are you saying you intended to harm them?

Seamus (*indignant*) They'd attacked us – ambushed us, messed up our clothes and that!

Prosecutor And you felt that gave you the right to take the law into your own hands?

Seamus Sure, it was no more than self-defence!

Prosecutor Oh? It sounds more like hot pursuit.

Seamus But they started it!

Janie (*indignant*) *You* started it – with them eggs!

Clerk Quiet, Jane!

Magistrate Well, Seamus, what do you say to that?

Seamus The eggs were only to stop vermin, sir.

Magistrate Vermin?

Seamus Something was nicking our eggs. Weasels, I thought, or else rats. (*he giggles*) Turned out to be two-legged ones.

The **Ryans** *all laugh in delight.*

Clerk Quiet!

Prosecutor (*stern*) Come, Seamus, let's have the truth.

Seamus *It is!*

Prosecutor Well I suggest you knew very well young Peter had been filching eggs from that nest, so you hit on this prank of filling a couple with castor oil and shampoo . . .

Seamus Never!

Mr Smith (*angry*) Admit it, you lying little brat! You tried to get us! (*This is the last straw for* **Mr Ryan** *who leans across to grab* **Mr Smith's** *jacket.*)

Mr Ryan You just say that to my face and see what you get!

Mr Smith (*pulling angrily free*) I will, mate, I will! Any time!

Clerk Mr Smith, Mr Ryan, unless you behave yourselves, you'll have to leave court.

Mr Smith Leave? (*To* **Mr Ryan**) Suits me just fine. You?

Mr Ryan (*jumping up in defiance*) You're on! (*At which the two men march out to do battle.*)

Mrs Ryan (*calling after them in alarm*) John you promised! *Briefly there is a general hubub of excitement from both families until . . .*

Clerk Quiet now! Settle down! (*he turns*) Do your worships have any questions?

Magistrate No thank you. (*pause*) Listen now, all of you. We find the case against all eight of you proved. (*There is a general groan of resentment before . . .*) Do any of them have a previous record?

Prosecutor Nothing, sir, no.

Magistrate Thank you. Usher, would you please try and get the fathers back into court. (*Pause as the usher leaves and the three magistrates whisper briefly.*) Stand up, all eight of you. Patrick Ryan, Katherine Ryan, Seamus Ryan, Sheena Ryan, Michael Ryan, Jane Smith, Leonard Smith, Peter Smith, you will each pay a fine of £5. Also we order that you all be bound over for a year to keep the peace in the sum of £20 each.

All eight react in alarm, shocked at such a vast

sum of money, not fully understanding. The two fathers return to court, both grinning broadly, neither showing signs of injury.

Magistrate   (*continued*) Mr Smith, Mr Ryan, if there is any more trouble between your two families within the next twelve months, we propose that all eight children should be brought back here and each should pay £20. It will be up to you parents to see that your children observe this order. (*pause*) You agree to their being bound over?

Mrs Ryan   With respect, your honours, it's not fair! Sure as anything, if there's any more trouble, them Smiths are the ones who'll start it!

Janie   *Us?*

Mrs Ryan   Yes, *you!*

Mr Ryan   (*to his wife*) Hang on now, love. (*He nods at* **Mr Smith**.) Him and me, we had a bit of a talk out there: we agreed to try and sort things out.

Mr Smith   That's right. Bury the hatchet, like.

Mrs Ryan   O, you did? And about time, too! A wicked shame you couldn't have come to it before they all ended up here in court.

Magistrate   May we take it, Mr and Mrs Ryan, that you agree?

Mr Ryan   Yes, sir.

Magistrate   Mr Smith, the same goes for you?

Mr Smith   Fair enough, aye.

Magistrate   Very well then, children, five pounds each now and you are each bound over to keep the peace and be of good behaviour – especially towards each other – in the sum of £20 for one year. Do you understand that? (*Pause as the children grunt and nod acceptance.*)
No more smoky bonfires, no filching, no more egg tricks, Seamus. (*pause*) Can the fines be paid now?

Mr Ryan   Yes, sir.

Mr Smith   Okay.

Magistrate   You two fathers can pay now, but you should take it out of whatever pocket-money the children receive.

Mr Ryan	They'll pay it, sir, never fear.
Mr Smith	Right.
Magistrate	Very well then, off you go, all of you. And from now on, be sure to behave like proper neighbours.

Questions for discussion and written work

Understanding the action

1 Why do you think the two families were so bitter towards each other?
2 What did you understand was meant by 'being bound over'? What else did the magistrates order?
3 Why do you think Mr Smith and his family felt out of luck?

Making up your mind

4 How would you try to avoid trouble if you had the Smiths as neighbours on one side and the Ryans on the other?
5 Do you think the ambush was reasonable retaliation for being tricked with doctored eggs? What retaliation, if any, would you have tried? Say why.
6 Talk about the advantages and disadvantages of having a large family of children like the Ryans. Discuss the responsibility, both at home and in terms of population.

Ideas for writing

7 Imagine you are a probation officer and write a report on the two families and the grievances dividing them.
8 Write a local newspaper report on the trial.
9 Write a letter of complaint to the local council about your nextdoor neighbours who you feel are making a deliberate nuisance of themselves.

Drama work

10 Improvise a scene as the two families leave court together — old enemies suddenly ordered to be friends.
11 Improvise a scene where you challenge the people nextdoor with being bad neighbours. Then turn it around so that they are now accusing you.
12 Improvise a scene between a policeman and the two families where he is trying to unscramble the cause of their fighting.

Flash-point

Trevor Wade, 15, is a sturdy, rowdy show-off who likes to be at the centre of attention in class.

Miss Frinton, 50, is a very keen teacher but is nick-named Flash-point because of her sharp temper with those she regards as noisy bullies like Trevor.

Carol Jones, 15, is Trevor's girlfriend, a 'punky' giggler.

Donald Green, 15, is an owl-like swot and Ms Frinton's favourite.

Mrs Wade is divorced and in the habit both of fussing and spoiling her son.

Also: **Janet**, (15), **Jenny** (15), **Headteacher**, **Police constable**, **Lawyer**, **Magistrate**, **Mrs James**.

Fade into end of chemistry practical. The rest of the class are leaving the lab as **Trevor**, *who is on report, goes to collect his card from Miss Frinton.*

Trevor	My report card, Miss.
Frinton	Oh yes.
Carol	(*calls*) Hey, Trev . . .
Trevor	Just coming.
Frinton	There you are.
Trevor	(*reading her comment*) 'Noisy and inattentive.' That's not fair!
Carol	(*in warning*) Trevor . . . .
Frinton	(dismissive) If you want good reports, do your homework, write up your experiments, and *try* instead of always shouting and showing off.
Trevor	I *do* try!
Frinton	Rubbish. Constantly disruptive. You only started chemistry at all because Carol's doing it.

Trevor	(*sulky*) Didn't . . .
Carol	(*brightly*) He's okay really, Miss.
Frinton	Then he can show it, Carol, by revising and doing well in the mocks next week. (**Trevor** *and* **Carol** *leave, talking together as they go to the next class.*)
Carol	You want to watch out with her.
Trevor	Flaming Flash-point!
Carol	You and her both, Trev. Sharp tongues and quick tempers.
Trevor	Frustrated, that's her trouble. Frustrated old spinster.
Carol	(*giggles*) You reckon she fancies you?
Trevor	(*snorts in contempt*) She's just looking for trouble.
Carol	Well don't you be the one to give it her or she'll have you out.
Trevor	Out where?
Carol	Out the school, you wallie, quick as light.
Trevor	You think that's what she's aiming at?
Carol	Could be. (*she shrugs*) Mind you, Trev, you do wind her up.

Fade to chemistry lab after the mocks. This time **Miss Frinton** *and* **Trevor** *are alone.*

Frinton	I'm sorry, Trevor, but that's final.
Trevor	(*angry*) But that's not . . . .
Frinton	(*interrupting*) Your results in the mocks show you don't stand a chance of getting a grade in the 16 + exam. There is no point in you entering for it.
Trevor	(*fiddling with one of the gas taps*) But look . . .
Frinton	(*interrupting*) Leave that gas-tap alone. You know you're not supposed to touch them.
Trevor	But I really need to have chemistry . . .
Frinton	(*interrupting*) Too late to think of that now.
Trevor	But . . .
Frinton	(*persisting*) You should have done some revision.
Trevor	(*again his hand goes to the gas tap*) I did revise . . .
Frinton	Will you *stop* fiddling with that gas-tap! *Now.* (*She hits irritably at his hand.*)

Trevor   (*explosive*) Get off! don't touch me again! *Ever!*

Fade to **Trevor's** *home that evening.*

Mrs Wade   But, Trevor, if you're going in for photography, you're going to need a pass in chemistry. I'm sure the careers master said . . .

Trevor   (*interrupting*) Look, mum whether I need it or not, there's no chance now. Orders of Ober-Sturm-Fuehrer Flashpoint. Verbotten! Finito!

Pause.

Trevor   Not a hope.

Mrs Wade   But why?

Trevor   Old Frinton's got the knife out for me, that's why.

Mrs Wade   What?

Trevor   Carol reckons she's trying to get me the boot.

Mrs Wade   (*alarmed*) From Oakleigh? But why?

Trevor   Vendetta, that's why. She has her favourites – the swots like Don Green and them – and her pet hates like me. I'm just a write-off to her. Just dole-queue junk

Fade to chemistry practical the next week.

Frinton   Trevor Wade, will you go and work where I told you.

Trevor   But Ronnie and me always go together.

Frinton   (*firm*) Not today. This acid experiment is too risky for me to be constantly keeping an eye on you.

Trevor   We'll be careful.

Frinton   No, I want you with someone reliable. Now go and work with Donald like I told you. (*pause*) Now I want all of you to remember how dangerous acid can be. You do *not* warm it over the bunsen burner the way Jenny's just started to do so. Hold on, Jenny, I'll just come and . . . (**Miss Frinton** *checks, realising* **Trevor** *has moved again.*) Trevor, for the *second* time, go and work with Donald!

Trevor   Look, I just want to talk to . . .

Frinton	Back over there. *Now.* (*pause*)
	Firstly, Jenny, use the tube-holder so you don't drop the test-tube when it gets hot. Now then, just watch . . .
Trevor	(*quietly to* **Donald**) Let's have that test-tube.
Donald	What?
Trevor	(*snatching it*) Give it here.
Donald	What are you doing? Hey you've broken it!
Trevor	(*calling out*) Miss! Breakage, Miss!
Frinton	(*to* **Jenny**) See how I keep the open end angled safely away so that, if the acid does spurt up . . .
Trevor	(*calls*) *Miss!*
Carol	Trev wants you, Miss.
Frinton	Just watch what I'm doing, Carol. Forget about Trevor Wade.
Trevor	(*calls*) Miss, I've broken me thingy! (*He climbs up on his lab stool and starts aping about.*)
Donald	Stop it, Trevor. Get down, you wallie!
Trevor	Shut up, you.
Frinton	(*calls*) Get down, Trevor.
Janet	(*interrupting*) Some more acid please, Miss.
Frinton	Stay at your place, Janet, I'll bring it over.
Trevor	(*calls*) Can't manage without me thingy, Miss!
Frinton	Get down off that stool, Trevor.
Jenny	You need to *shout* at him, Miss.
Frinton	(*moving towards him*) Trevor, get *down* . . . (*She emphasises the command by waving angrily at him with her free hand.* **Trevor** *reacts, lurching back with an indignant cry.*)
Trevor	Hey! (*He swings his arms wildly around to keep from falling, one hand striking the teacher violently across the side of the face.* **Miss Frinton** *lurches heavily back against the nearest lab bench. The acid bottle breaks against it, splashing her with acid as she goes down on the floor.*)
Trevor	Watch out! (*He clambers off the stool, going to her.*) Here, you okay?

Frinton	Monster! Get back!
Trevor	But . . .
Frinton	*Back!*
Donald	Watch out for all that acid!
Janet	I'll fetch Mrs James.
Carol	Here, that's blood!
Jenny	She's all cut, look.
Donald	I'll help you, Miss.
Frinton	I'll manage. Just run lots of water to swamp all this spilt acid.
Jack	What happened?
Jenny	He hit her.
Trevor	Just – an *accident* . . .
Donald	*Liar* . . .
Trevor	It *was!* Carol, you saw.
Carol	That's right, yeah. An accident.
Frinton	Jack, go and get Mrs McKendrick. Quick as you can.
Donald	You're still bleeding, Miss.
Frinton	Yes, it'll need stitching.
Mrs James	Good heavens, what happened?
Frinton	Trevor Wade hit me. Knocked me over.

Fade to head's office next morning.

Mrs Wade	Suspended?
Head	For the time being, yes.
Mrs Wade	Outrageous. You have no right.
Head	An assault on a teacher, Mrs Wade. Extremely serious.
Mrs Wade	Except that it was an *accident*. Right, Trevor?
Trevor	Yeah – definitely.
Head	I'm fully aware of Trevor's version.
Mrs Wade	Not just Trevor's. I've talked to his classmates. They all confirm it.
Head	Mrs Wade, Trevor is suspended until the special meeting of the panel next week and that is final.

Mrs Wade	*She pushed him!* That Frinton woman hit him to get him down off the stool. She's the one who ought to be suspended, not Trevor!
	Pause.
Head	Mrs Wade, your son's past record of indiscipline . . .
Mrs Wade	(*interrupting*) That's not proof of anything. I insist you take him back. Now.
	Pause.
Head	Well if so, there'll have to be an independent investigation by the police – who just might decide to prosecute.
Mrs Wade	What?
Head	It's your decision.

Fade to police station next day. A police constable interviewing **Trevor** *while his mother listens.*

Constable	Once again, please, Trevor, to make sure I've got the details down right. Start from where you broke the test-tube.
Trevor	Okay, it's one of her rules in chemi prac: if you break anything you have to report it straight away. She's supposed to come over, see how it got broken and that. But when I started calling her, she took no notice.
Constable	And that's when you got up on the stool?
Trevor	Well yeah – to catch her attention.
Constable	(*writing it down*) To catch her attention.
Trevor	You see, because it was *me* calling, she had to go and make out she hadn't heard. Typical. See, she's got it in for me and . . .
Constable	(*interrupting*) Just the facts, please. What happened next?
Trevor	Well, at last she started across, but instead of asking what's up, she yelled at me to *get down* and

	took this great shove at me. Took me by surprise – caught me off balance. Okay, next thing, she dodged back and clobbered into the bench.
Constable	Yes?
Trevor	Well, she was holding this acid bottle and it got smashed. Cut her hand – acid all over the place. So naturally I nipped down to help her. But, well, she pushed me away. Called me a mad animal or something
Constable	Oh? Why should she do that, Trevor, if it all happened the way you just said?

Fade to school, **Trevor** *and* **Carol** *talking to* **Donald Green**.

Donald	(*surprised*) Flippin heck, I didn't know the police were onto it.
Trevor	They wouldn't have been except the head goon wanted to blame me – making out I *meant* to hit her. Anyway, it's no sweat because everyone else saw it wasn't like that – saw it was an accident.
Donald	Oh. Well – er . . .
Carol	Of course it was, Donald. You saw old Flash-point shove him.
Donald	I didn't think she actually touched you, Trevor.
Trevor	Of course she did. Why else should I swing around like that?
Donald	You see, I thought . . .
Carol	Yeah? What?
Donald	Well, that Trevor was pretending – putting that on.
Trevor	*Why?* What was there to pretend about?
Donald	Er . . .
Trevor	She shoved me – made me lose my balance. Okay? *Pause.*
Donald	If you say so.
Trevor	You say so, too, Donald old son. There's no sense any of us telling it differently to the police.
Donald	Oh.
Carol	Of course there isn't, you whimp.

Pause.

Trevor Okay then? Accident?

Pause.

Donald Okay.

Trevor Right. Same as the way that test-tube got broken.

Donald What?

Carol Maybe you didn't see how it happened.

Donald Yes I did. Trev took it from me and . . .

Trevor (*interrupting*) Dropped it by accident.

Donald Oh.

Trevor (*menacing*) I don't think you did see it, old son. Okay?

Donald (*after a pause*). Okay.

Fade to courtroom. **Miss Frinton** *is giving evidence.*

Frinton I again ordered him off the stool and then gestured. He gave this wild bellow and struck out at me – hit me across the side of the face – knocked me completely off balance. Then he jumped down and, just for a moment, I thought he was going to hit me again. But then – well I think he began to realise what he'd done – my cuts, all the blood, the acid and soforth.

Lawyer Miss Frinton, you say you gestured. Might you have *touched* him when you did that?

Frinton Definitely not, no.

Lawyer Is it true you are known to your pupils as Flash-point?

Frinton (*frowns*) So I've heard.

Lawyer Do you know why that might be?

Frinton To do with practicals on hydrocarbons, I imagine. When we measure their various flashpoints.

Lawyer Oh? Nothing to do with your temperament? (*Pause.* **Miss Frinton** *shrugs but stays silent.*)

Lawyer (*continued*) You see, I'm asking if this incident really happened in quite the way you've described.

Frinton	It did.
Lawyer	You had a tricky experiment to oversee, you saw Trevor call to you from up on his lab stool; and you reached, er, flashpoint, yes? You shouted at him to get down and then you enforced it by giving him a push . . .
Frinton	No. He hit me. Quite deliberately – as I just said.
Lawyer	It isn't that, through your dislike of Trevor Wade, your memory is playing you false?
Frinton	No. I wrote it all down that same day in the Accident Book, so I'm quite certain.

Fade to later – **Trevor** *now in the witness box.*

Lawyer	Trevor, how did the test-tube get broken?
Trevor	Can't remember.
Lawyer	When you got up on the stool, wasn't it really because you wanted to put on an act?
Trevor	You what?
Lawyer	To amuse your mates.
Trevor	No. I was trying to get her attention about the breakage.
Lawyer	Well I suggest you were up there solely to lark about.
Trevor	No.
Lawyer	And when Miss Frinton ignored these absurd antics of yours, you saw that it would mean losing face in front of your mates.
Trevor	I don't understand . . .
Lawyer	Wasn't it because of that you suddenly saw red and lashed out at her?
Trevor	*No*. It was an accident, like I said.

Fade to later. **Carol** *is now in the witness box.*

Carol	So then old Flash-point – er, sorry, Miss Frinton – she takes the bottle and goes off to Janet. Okay, just as she's passing Trev, I saw her take this great

	shove at him – like, to push him down off the stool.
Lawyer	You saw that clearly? An actual push?
Carol	Yeah! Then Miss dodged back against the bench and fell. Then, when Trev nipped down to help her, she yelled at him, making out she was scared, making out he was to blame.
Lawyer	Whyever should she do that?
Carol	Obvious. Because she's got it in for him. She's always picking on him. Real vendetta.

Fade to later. **Donald** *is now in the witness box.*

Lawyer	So, Donald, you thought you saw Miss Frinton push at Trevor, causing him to lose his balance and accidentally hit her, is that it?
Donald	Well, er, yes, I suppose so.
Lawyer	How did the test-tube get broken?
Donald	(*mutters*) Er . . . (**Donald** *glances at* **Trevor** *who shakes his head.*)
Lawyer	Don't look at Trevor now. You are giving evidence to the magistrates, not to him.
Donald	Er, I didn't see how.
	Tense pause.
Lawyer	Donald, would you expect the magistrates to be aware of the kind of pressures which youngsters like you and Carol can face from their classmates? From boys they meet everyday in class and hence are obliged to get along with?
	Pause. **Donald** *stares in silence.*
Lawyer	(*continued*) Has Trevor Wade ever threatened you?
	Pause. **Donald** *is unable to speak.*
Lawyer	(*continued*) Donald, you do realise what it means to be under oath? That lying in this court is an offence just as serious as the one Trevor is charged with?
Donald	(*near to panic*) Yes.
Lawyer	And have you so far been truthful with this court? (*pause*) Might you have twisted your evidence somewhat so as to help a classmate?

Pause. **Donald** *gestures in shame and fear.*

Donald   Yes . . .

Lawyer   Would you like to tell the magistrates again what
you remember of the incident
Donald *nods in relief.*

Donald   You see, to begin with, he was angry with Miss
Frinton because she kept sending him back to
work with me. So when he came back the second
time, he grabbed the test-tube from me and then
smashed it. Deliberately. Then he started yelling
out to her and waving the broken bits. Next he got
up on his stool and started raving on – showing off
as usual. Next thing, Miss Frinton came across, told
him to get down and waved at him. But instead he
gave this wild yell and acted it up that she'd made
him lose his balance. He flung around and hit her on
the side of the face.

*Fade to later – the magistrates now outside
discussing their verdict.*

Carol   (*to* **Donald**) Rotten little traitor!

Donald   Shut up!

Trevor   Why'd you say all that?

Donald   What?

Trevor   Trying to drop me in it – saying all that about me
acting up.

Donald   You were! As usual!

Trevor   Not about losing my balance. Not then I wasn't!

Donald   Well that's how it looked to me!

Carol   Rubbish!

Donald   Look, Carol, I was stood right beside him. He
deliberately made out he was off balance so as to
. . .

Trevor   (*interrupting*) It was an accident like I said.

Donald   (*scornful*) Oh yes . . .

Trevor   Yes!

Donald   Well then, why'd you threaten me?

Trevor   You what?

Donald	At school – before I spoke to the police.
Trevor	(guffaws) Who are you kidding . . . (*he stops as the lawyer calls out.*)
Lawyer	(*calls*) Stand in court!
	Pause as the three magistrates return.
Lawyer	(*continued*) Trevor, remain standing.
Magistrate	Trevor Neil Wade, we find the case against you proved.

Fade to several weeks later, once again in court.

Magistrate	From the head's report on you, Trevor, we note that you have now been transferred to another school. We very much hope you will use that move as an opportunity to start afresh, keep out of trouble and learn to get on with people. (*pause*) Now then, because this is your first trouble in court, we shan't be sending you away to a detention centre. Instead we order that you be put on probation for twelve months. Now this isn't a let-off. You'll have to report regularly and comply with the various conditions. If you fail to do so – to the letter – you could be brought back again to the court to be dealt with.

Questions for discussion and written work

☐☐

Understanding the action

1 Before Donald changed his evidence in court, did you think Trevor was guilty or not of assaulting Miss Frinton? Give your reasons.
2 Why was it that Miss Frinton made Trevor sit with Donald in the chemistry practical instead of with his normal partner?
3 Why do you think Trevor broke the test-tube and then made such a fuss in the class?

Making up your mind

4 How do you think a teacher should handle a disruptive pupil?
5 What steps would you take if you felt that a fellow pupil had a vendetta against you and was set on landing you in real trouble?
6 If you had been a close witness to the incident, how would you have reacted? Would you have felt you owed more loyalty to Trevor or to the teacher or to the truth? Talk about whether Carol's loyalty should have been any different from Donald's.

Ideas for writing

7 Imagine that you are a probation officer and write a background report on Trevor.
8 Write a scene where Trevor and his mother discuss whether it will be for the best to let the school deal with him or whether they should get the police involved.
9 Write a report for the local newspaper on Trevor's trial.

Drama work

10 Improvise a scene in the lab where a couple of pupils quietly try to get two others more and more wound up. Then replay it the other way round.
11 Improvise a scene between the three magistrates arguing whether Trevor should be fined; be sent to a detention centre; be ordered to spend twenty four hours at an attendance centre; be made to work for twenty hours community service; be put on probation for a year.
12 Improvise a scene discussing the details of a classroom assault, knowing that you may soon be called as a witness in court.

Firebug

Dave Blackburn, 13, wants to be a speedway rider and is forever scrambling his mini-motorcycle around the local woods. He is a selfish lad who likes to get his own way.

Rita Blackburn, 12, is just as thoughtless as her older brother and is every bit as fast as a scrambles rider.

Mr Middleton is the burly, outraged farmer who owns the woods.

Freddy Tallis is a dirty old tramp who loves the woods and resents noisy kids who roar around disturbing them.

Mr Blackburn is a busy, over-worked garage owner.

The defence lawyer is a stout, pompous, country solicitor.

The court reporter has a sharp mind and seems to find most things funny.

The police constable is a peacemaker who tries his best to stay neutral.

Also: **Prosecuting lawyer**, **Magistrate**, **Judge**.

> *Dave and Rita are competing against each other in a wild motorcycle race along the woodland paths. They roar into a muddy bend, corner fast, only to crash slap into a pile of branches pulled dangerously across to block the track.*

Dave	(*alarmed*) Watch out!
Rita	(*shouts*) Can't stop!
Dave	(*hurt*) Ouch!
Rita	Sorry! Hey, you okay?
Dave	Look at the bike!
	*Pause as **Rita** helps him pull his bike clear of the branches.*
Rita	Whoever dragged all these across the track has got to be a total lunatic!

Dave	I bet it's that same old bloke as before.
Rita	That old weirdo? (*She breaks off as* **Tallis** *shouts nearby.*)
Tallis	(*abrupt*) Devils! (*He starts flinging things.*) Off with you!
Rita	(*hit by a clod of earth*) Ow! That hurt!
Tallis	And what about all the pheasants you scare off? The little munt-jack deers?
Dave	Stop flinging things!
Tallis	Then be off with you!
Dave	We've as much right here as you!
Tallis	Devils . . .
Rita	Come on, he's bonkers.
Tallis	Vandals!
Dave	(*hit by a log*) Ouch!
Tallis	Destroyers of nature!
Dave	Come on . . .

Fade to later. Once again, with much revving of their mini-motorcycles, the two race round a bend and then slither to an emergency stop. This time the path is blocked by a landrover. Farmer **Middleton** *standing angrily beside it.*

Middleton	(*angry*) Right, you two – out of these woods – *now* – for good!
Dave	(*sharp*) You can't stop us coming in here!
Rita	This is a public footpath.
Middleton	(*still angry*) Except you never stick to it.
Rita	(*sharp*) We do!
Middleton	Tyre marks everywhere . . .
Dave	(*mutters*) There's other kids ride around in here, too.
Middleton	(*sharp*) Rubbish. Only you two Blackburn tearaways.
Rita	Not just us . . .
Middleton	(*persisting*) You're the ones I saw pulling down the footpath notices.

Dave	(*angry*) Liar!
Middleton	(*flaring*) Oh aye? (*He belts* **Dave** *hard across the ear.*) Well see if *that* feels like a lie!
Dave	(*in pain*) Hey!
Middleton	Cheeky little brat. Now get out of here!
Dave	(*going*) We'll be back!
Middleton	Is that a threat?
Rita	You've got no right!
Middleton	(*shouting after them*) So tell that to the police. They'll be round to see you soon as I can get to a telephone!

Fade to later at the **Blackburn** *home.*

Mr Blackburn	The public have a right to go through those woods, constable.
Constable	But *only* along the main footpath, sir.
Dave	The farmer can't prove we've ridden anywhere else!
Constable	Someone has, David – someone with tyre treads which, by an odd stroke of chance, happen to match your bikes.
	Pause.
Mr Blackburn	Well, you two?
Dave	Maybe we did sort of miss the track once or twice, but . . .
Constable	That's trespass, David, just the moment you're off that footpath.
Dave	But . . .
Constable	(*persisting*) Whether or not that was you who tore down his notices, the farmer's of a mood to take you to court.
Dave	(*indignant*) Then we'll take *him* to court for hitting me!
Constable	Boxed your ears, was how Mr Middleton described it, on account of you calling him a liar.
Dave	He really laid into me!

Rita	And what about that mad farmworker of his! He could have *killed* us today.
Dave	Yes! Piling all those branches across the path!
Rita	Then flinging things at us.
Constable	I don't know ought about him. Nor am I saying you can't go up there. So long as you wheel them two bikes alongside the road until you get into the woods, that's legal by me. but you set tread off of that public footpath again and you'll be in dead trouble with the farmer.

Fade to woodland, a few days later. The two are once again back with their mini-motorcycles.

Dave	Round the scrambles course, okay?
Rita	Don't be daft. Suppose old Middleton hears us.
Dave	Okay, you hang on here and keep a watch out for him while I go round.

*Pause, as **Dave** races off through the trees while **Rita** moves to the edge of the wood to peer across the fields. What she sees sends her rushing back to wave **Dave** down as he completes the circuit.*

Rita	Quiet! (*Pauses for him to cut his engine.*) He's just across at the old barn. Look.

Pause, as they creep to the edge to peer across.

Dave	I can't see him.
Rita	He was there by the Landrover. (*pause*) Look, there he is, just running out of the barn.
Dave	Think he could have heard the bike?
Rita	Don't know. When I saw him before, he was heaving that big jerry-can out the back of the Landrover and . . . *Hey! Look!*
Dave	Smoke!
Rita	Flames, too, look!
Dave	Looks like the whole barn . . .
Rita	Flippin' heck!
Dave	And he's just watching it. Just letting it burn!
Rita	See there – someone round the other side and all.

Dave	Looks like that old farmworker of his.
Rita	Running off . . .
Dave	Here, watch out, Middleton's seen us!
Rita	You what?
Dave	He was looking straight up here – jumped in the truck and – he's coming, look!
Rita	Oh heck . . .
Dave	Come on! *Run!*
	Pause, as the two race back to the motorcycles and go to start them up.
Rita	(*breathless*) Hang it . . .
Dave	What's up?
Rita	My crash-helmet! I left it by the hedge.
Dave	(*revving his bike*) Too late now!
Middleton	(*calls*) Hey! You two!
Dave	Come on . . .
	The two roar away through the trees as . . .
Middleton	(*calls*) Stop! Couple of damned firebugs!

Fade, to later at the **Blackburn's** *home.*

Mr Blackburn	You two are very quiet. (*pause*) Something wrong?
Dave	You see, er . . .
	He gulps at the sound of a knock on the door.
Rita	The door . . .
Mr Blackburn	Well go on then.
	Pause, as **Dave** *goes to answer it.*
Constable	Your dad in, is he?
Dave	Through here.
Constable	(*formal*) Mr Blackburn, I've questions for Dave and Rita, if that's all right with you.
Mr Blackburn	(*worried*) What about?
Constable	Farmer Middleton's barn, sir, the one up near the woods. It caught fire today. Burnt to the ground.
Mr Blackburn	(*alarmed*) What!
	The **Constable** *turns to the two children.*
Constable	David and Rita, you don't have to say anything unless you wish to do so, but whatever you do say

	may be put in writing and used in evidence. All right? Where were you around midday today?
Dave	Er – midday?
Rita	Twelve o'clock . . .?
Dave	Not sure . . .
Constable	Out with those mini-motorcycles of yours, were you?
	Pause.
Mr Blackburn	Well go on, you know you were.
Constable	Let them answer, please, sir.
Dave	(*to the* **Constable**) Yes.
Constable	Whereabouts (*pause*) Up the woods, were you?
Dave	For a while.
Constable	Did you go anywhere near the barn?
Dave	*No.*
Constable	You're sure?
Dave	Yes!
Constable	Rita?
Rita	*No.*
Constable	You have crash-helmets?
	Pause.
Mr Blackburn	Of course they do.
Constable	Got them here?
Dave	Er – only one. (*pause*) Lost the other.
Constable	Colour?
Dave	Sort of yellow . . .
	Pause, as the **Constable** *takes the lost crash-helmet from a bag.*
Constable	This one?
Dave	(*mutters*) Er – could be . . .
Constable	Found by Mr Middleton this afternoon near his barn.
Rita	(*abrupt*) Wasn't . . .
Constable	He says he saw you drop it, Rita. He says you dropped it when he caught the pair of you running away from the burning barn.

Fade, to lawyer's office.
(*The* **lawyer** *has only agreed to defend* **Dave** *and*

Rita *in court because he is a friend of their dad.*)

Lawyer	(*solemn*) So, Rita, from the way Mr Middleton was heaving this big jerry-can into the barn, it looked to be heavy – in other words, full, yes?
Rita	Very – yes. Then empty when he came running out with it and tossed it into the back of his Landrover.
Dave	Then almost straight off, there was this great whoosh. Almost like a bomb going off.
Rita	And all the time, he just stood there *watching* it.
Dave	Except when he caught sight of us up the edge of the wood.
Rita	He came roaring up after us. Headlights on, hooting like billy-o.
Dave	A raving nutter.
Lawyer	Except, David, he isn't a nutter. He's a well-known local farmer with no reason to go and burn down his own barn.
Dave	(*indignant*) He did it!
Rita	We *saw* him!
Lawyer	Whereas he's saying he *saw* you. And what's more, he saw you burning it just a few days after you'd threatened him.
Dave	Eh?
Lawyer	Because he'd boxed your ears and chased you out of the woods.
Dave	He'd right laid into me!
Lawyer	Maybe. But it's best you shouldn't say too much about that in court.
Dave	Why?
Lawyer	The magistrates may feel you decided to burn his barn down out of spite.
Rita	But we didn't!
Lawyer	The court prosecutor will say you did.
Rita	(*shrill*) You – you don't believe us, do you! You think we did burn it!
Lawyer	(*solemn*) Whether I do or not is unimportant, young woman. I've agreed to represent your case and

	that's what I shall do.
Rita	But . . .
Lawyer	(*persisting*) However, it's only fair to say that I'm none too hopeful of getting you off.

Fade, to their trial in the juvenile court. Present are the farmer, the children and their parents, the magistrates and lawyers and also a press reporter.

Middleton	Seeing the smoke, I drove across and, as I got near, I saw these two dash from the barn – off like a brace of rabbits for the wood. I tried to head them off, but they were too quick. So then I swung back to try and extinguish the fire – no luck. Total loss. Tragedy. Fine old building like that.
Magistrate	A listed ancient building, I believe.
Middleton	Yes, sir. Dated back hundreds of years. Irreplacable.
Prosecutor	And you recognised these two at the time?
Middleton	You see, near the barn I picked up one of their crash-helmets. Mind, I'd have known them without that, young devils.
Prosecutor	With whom you've had frequent trouble in the past?
Middleton	I have, aye. Cheeking me, calling me a liar, threatening me – and finally coming to torch my barn!

Fade, to later in court – **Dave** *now giving evidence.*

Dave	I didn't threaten him! Just said we'd be back.
Prosecutor	Meaning what?
Dave	To scramble our bikes around the woods.
Prosecutor	You're sure? Sure it wasn't to do with vengeance? Not said maliciously?
Dave	(*indignant*) *No.* Look, if anyone was malicious, it was *him!*

Prosecutor	The farmer? How?
Dave	Well, like, he used to send this old farmworker of his to fling things at us and pull branches out across the track. Dead dangerous.
Prosecutor	But, David, Mr Middleton employs *no* farmworkers. None.
Dave	(*indignant*) He does. We saw him at the barn – saw him helping to burn it down.
Prosecutor	Oh?
Dave	He dashed out the back just as the flames went up.
Prosecutor	Did you mention that to the police?
Dave	(*awkward*) Er – I can't remember. Not sure.
Prosecutor	A witness to what you *say* happened and yet you're not sure?
Dave	What was the point? He was helping him – helping the farmer.
Prosecutor	So you say . . .
Dave	He was!
Prosecutor	Except you have no proof of it and you didn't tell the police.
	Pause.
Prosecutor	(*continued*) Well, David, I suggest you're telling the court a pack of lies.
Dave	What?
Prosecutor	(*hard*) I suggest the two of you went out of spite and set light to the barn . . .
Dave	No!
Prosecutor	(*persisting*) And then, because the farmer suddenly drove up and saw you running off, you dreamed up this unlikely tale about seeing him burn down his own barn.
Dave	No! We saw him do it!
Prosecutor	Just as you saw this non-existent farmworker?
Dave	Yes!
Prosecutor	Then, if so, David, why run away when the farmer spotted you?
Dave	(*flustered*) Well . . . like . . .
Prosecutor	Hardly the action of innocent bystanders, surely?

Dave   (*rattled*) Look, he'd hit me before and – and he was racing up at us, hooting and that. Anyone would have run!

Prosecutor   Anyone, David? Or anyone just caught red-handed setting light to a man's barn?

Fade to later, the magistrates now out of court discussing their verdict. The two Blackburn children are talking to the press reporter.

Reporter   Did you two know about that old barn?

Dave   It wasn't us burnt it!

Reporter   (*laughs*) Okay.

Rita   Honestly!

Reporter   Parts of it dated right back to Tudor times and it had a preservation order on it.

Dave   What's that mean?

Reporter   That the farmer was supposed by law to keep it in good repair. A *very* costly duty.

Rita   You – er – you mean . . .

Reporter   A tragic loss historically. But I suspect Mr Middleton is happy enough to collect the insurance and be rid of it.

Dave   (*shocked*) Hey, but that's . . . (*he breaks off as . . .*)

Prosecutor   Stand in court.

The magistrates return.

Magistrate   Remain standing, you two. David Blackburn, Rita Blackburn, (*pause*) we find the case against you proved.

The two youngsters gasp at the injustice.

Magistrate   Does either have any previous court record?

Prosecutor   No, sir.

Magistrate   Thank you, David and Rita, the case will be adjourned for three weeks so that background reports can be prepared on you. You will be back here at ten o'clock on the 24th when we shall decide on sentence.

Fade, to later outside the court.

Reporter Hey, that old farmworker you mentioned – what does he look like?

Dave Tatty old clothes, dirty beard . . .

Rita He wears a flat hat.

Reporter With the peak facing backwards?

Rita Yes.

Reporter (*laughs*) I thought so.

Rita What's so funny?

Reporter That's Freddie Tallis, a local tramp. I did a piece on him once for the paper.

Dave He was definitely there at the barn.

Reporter Well, if so, he wasn't helping Mr Middleton like you thought. He's no friend of the farmers – nor anyone else.

Rita He once hit me with a big clod of earth.

Reporter (*laughs*) I can believe it. Even so, it's worth trying to find him.

Rita (*alarmed*) What?

Reporter Well, if he's a witness to what really happened . . .

Dave He is!

Reporter Okay then, try those old brickworks along past the wood. That's where I last saw him.

Fade to brickworks next day.

Rita Dead creepy here, Dave . . .

Dave (*scared*) Stupid . . .

Rita We should have told dad – got him to come.

Dave Silly . . .

Rita But supposing . . .

Dave (*urgent*) Listen . . .

Rita What?

Dave Footsteps. (*calls*) Mr Tallis! (*pause*) Along here.

Rita I'm not going down there!

Dave Okay. (*pause*) Stay here alone.

Rita	No!
Dave	That reporter said he was okay really.
Rita	Just odd!
Dave	Yeah . . . well . . .
Rita	(*scared*) Let's forget it, Dave. Let's go home.
Dave	Don't be stupid. (*calls*) Mr Tallis!
Tallis	(*nearby*) Get away!
Rita	(*startled*) Ah!
Dave	Er . . . excuse me, sir . . .
Tallis	Get off with you, plaguing hounds!
Dave	(*urgent*) But, please, you were there.
Rita	At the barn.
Dave	When it burnt down.
Tallis	(*sharp*) No!
Rita	We saw you!
Tallis	Never. Never anywhere near there.
Dave	You were! You used to fling things at us!
Rita	Pull branches across . . .
Tallis	(*abrupt*) What you expect? Young devils, fouling them lovely woods! Devils on bike-back!
Rita	That's not fair!
Dave	Only having a bit of *fun*.
Tallis	Fun? Roaring and screaming? You made the sparrow-hawk desert her young! Used to be little munt-jack deers up them woods until you two come with your infernal noise and fumes!
Rita	Please, mister, we didn't know!
Tallis	Of course you didn't! Know nothing, *care* for nothing – nothing of nature, nothing of the woodlands save only your damned right of way. Devils on bikes.
Rita	Please, mister . . . we don't want to go to prison!
Tallis	Eh? What you on about?
Rita	That's where they'll send us if you don't help!
Dave	Detention centre.
Tallis	Oh-ah? Best place for you. All the noise you want in there – clanging and shouting, crowding and shoving!
Rita	Please, mister . . .

Tallis	No! You don't care, so why should I?
Dave	(*urgent*) That farmer, he said it was *us*.
Tallis	(*scowling*) Farmer?
Dave	Old Middleton – the liar.
Tallis	That farmer – he's worse even than what you two are! Destroyer of nature. Tried to burn me alive, he did.
Rita	Yes!
Dave	In the barn.
Rita	We were watching.
Dave	We saw you scrambling out.
Rita	We thought you'd been helping him.
Dave	Will you help us?
Rita	Just come and tell them . . .
Dave	Please!

Fade to the Appeal Court where a judge is hearing the fresh evidence as the **Blackburn** *children listen with their* **father**.

Tallis	I was asleep in there, me lord.
Lawyer	In the barn?
Tallis	That's right. I heard him drive up outside, then saw him come in with this big jerry-can.
Judge	Saw whom?
Tallis	Farmer Middleton, me lord. He poured stuff onto the hay bales not far from where I was snugged down. Then he lit her up. Damnee, Tallis, I thought, the devil's here to roast you alive.
Judge	Roast, Mr Tallis?
Tallis	Ah well, me lord, I realised I was wrong on that. Not murder. Just a simple case of insure-and-burn, then blame it on them two noisy tear-aways.
Lawyer	What happened after he lit the hay bales?
Tallis	Naturally, he run off outside. So then I made off out the back way – ran clear and left him to his mischief.

Fade to later in court.

Judge The evidence from this new witness clearly confirms what the Blackburn children said about the farmer setting light to his own barn that day. (*pause*) Accordingly, we order that their conviction for arson be set aside . . .

Fade to later.

Dave What'll happen to old Middleton?

Lawyer He'll be charged with lying under oath, with making a fraudulent insurance claim on the barn, and with deliberately destroying a building listed for its special historical value.

Tallis Ah – and that's more of a happy ending than you two plaguing varmits deserve!

Rita Why?

Tallis Who'll help the sparrow-hawk and them little deer you scared off, eh? Who'll care for them?

Questions for discussion and written work

□ □

Understanding the action

1 Why was it so important for the Blackburn children to find the tramp?
2 Why did the farmer decide to burn down his own barn?
3 Why was the crash-helmet important in the story?

Making up your mind

4 Imagine you are a person who owns quiet woodlands rich in wildlife. What would you do if kids started roaring round them on motorcycles?
5 Do you think the farmer was right to hit Dave for being cheeky and calling him a liar?
6 How do you feel about tramps and vagrants? Would you welcome one into your street or allow one to sleep in your garden shed?

Ideas for writing

7 Write a letter to your parents explaining why you have decided to leave home and started living rough like a tramp.
8 Write a news report on the children's successful appeal hearing.
9 Write a scene where the three magistrates are discussing whether or not the Blackburn kids had burnt down the barn – and then deciding on the sentence.

Drama work

10 Improvise a scene where you and a friend have been wrongly accused of a serious crime. Play it firstly with the investigating police constable secondly with your parents.
11 Improvise a scene where the farmer tells his wife he has decided to burn down his barn then goes on to discuss whether to try and blame it on the tramp or the children or an accident.
12 Improvise two scenes where you and your lawyer are planning your defence in a forthcoming trial:
    (a) where you are innocent but the lawyer doesn't believe you.
    (b) where you are guilty but the lawyer thinks you are innocent.

Cannibal

□ □

Leslie Martin, 13, is a black boy who has the quiet solemness of someone who knows that the days of the world are numbered.

Garry Martin, also 13 and also black, is Leslie's adopted brother. He is all fizz, fuss and fire.

Stewart Watson, 12, is titchy and wide-eyed, a teachers' pet and sly as they come.

Frank Blair, 14, is built like a barrel with arms and legs but very little brain.

Tony Rawlins, 14, is an owl-like swot with large spectacles and an earnest manner.

The police constable, although young, is very worldly-wise about BMX thieving.

Also: **Mr Martin, Magistrate, Prosecuting lawyer, Mrs Watson.**

□ □

Fade into BMX riding at the local club. **Garry** *is just completing a circuit on their new BMX and is cheered on by* **Leslie.**

Leslie	That was great the way you zapped out of the burn.
Garry	You reckon?
Leslie	Terrific, man.
Constable	Hey, you two lads, is that your bike?
	The two **Martin** *boys react as the* **Constable** *comes up to them with* **Tony.**
Constable	(*continued*) I'll just take a look at it, okay?
Leslie	What?
Garry	Why?
Constable	I'm informed that it could be stolen property.
Garry	What?
Constable	Stolen, lad. Nicked, okay?

Garry	No way!
Leslie	Shut it, Garry.
Garry	He needs a warrant!
Leslie	He doesn't. Go ahead, sir, take a look.
Garry	(*to* **Tony**) Hey, is this why you were poking around earlier?
Tony	(*flustered*) Look, it's mine – my bike! Okay, so it's been cannibalised. Different wheels and saddle. But definitely my frame.
Constable	(*turns from bike*) All right, you two, where did you get it from?
Leslie	We bought it.
Garry	Paid good money.
Constable	When?
Leslie	Just last week.
Constable	Did you do the respray job?
Leslie	No.
Garry	We bought it like that.
Leslie	Just as it is.
Constable	Who from?
Garry	A mate.
Constable	Name?
Garry	Can't remember.
Constable	(*doubting*) Oh yes . . .
Leslie	Don't be so daft, Garry.
Garry	Not daft!
Leslie	We bought it off of Stewart Watson, sir. Him and Frank Blair. Paid them forty-two quid for it.
Constable	Where do they live?
Leslie	Stewart's is the end house down Linton Avenue.
Constable	And you two are?
Leslie	Leslie and Garry Martin, 18 Wurley Road.
Constable	Right then, off home and tell your parents what's up, then get them to come down the station with you later on. Meanwhile, I'll take charge of the bike.
Garry	You *what?*
Constable	You see this number etched on the underside of the peddle housing here? Those are Tony's initials and

postcode. I know because I marked them there myself last month as part of our Bike Watch scheme. Right, I'll see you with your parents after I've checked with these other two lads.

Fade, to later at the **Watson** *home.*

Mrs Watson	In the old garage, constable. This way.
Constable	I'd like you to be present, Mrs Watson, since there's a suspicion of theft.
Mrs Watson	O dear. All right then. (*She shows him into the garage where Stewart and Frank are working on BMX parts.*) Stewart and Frank use it as a workshop.
Constable	Looks more like a factory to me. Where'd you get all these BMX bits from, lads?
Stewart	Er, mostly down the BMX club.
Constable	(*doubting*) Oh yes? There must be enough frames and parts in here for half a dozen bikes. (*pause*) Which of you is Stewart?
Stewart	I am.
Constable	Well, Stewart, like I just told your mum, I'm here about a stolen BMX, and I have reason to believe you two may be involved. Now then, you're not obliged to say anything unless you wish to do so, but whatever you do say may be put in writing and used in evidence. Understood?
Stewart	Yes.
Constable	Frank?
Frank	Right, gov.
Constable	Did you sell a Burner BMX to Leslie and Garry Martin last week?
Stewart	No.
Constable	You're sure.
Stewart	Yes!
Constable	They said you took £42 off them for it.
Stewart	They're lying.
Constable	Why should they do that?
Frank	Dunno.
Stewart	(*quickly*) They're trying to put the blame onto us, that's why.

Constable	All right then, so what about this Aladdin's cave full of stuff – all these parts and wheels and frames you've got here? You got it all from the BMX club, you say?
Frank	Yeah . . .
Stewart	No.
Constable	Make up your minds.
Stewart	It was Les and Garry. They brought all the stuff here – said we were to clean up all the bits and then make them up into whole bikes.
Constable	Did they say where they got all these parts?
Stewart	Yes. From their dad. They said he works as a dustman and collects them as scrap on his rounds.
Constable	(*doubting*) Scrap?
Stewart	Yes!
Frank	That's right, gov.
Constable	Come on now, lads, none of these bits look much like dustcart junk to me.
Frank	We cleaned them up, okay?
Constable	A lot of them look brand new.
Frank	Yeah.
Stewart	We resprayed the frames.
Constable	So I can see. (*pause*) Stewart, why did you start off by telling me you'd got all this stuff from the BMX club?
Stewart	Because – well, you see, because they'd threatened us – Les and Garry – they told us to do up the parts or else.
Constable	So you were scared of naming them, is that it?
Stewart	Yes. Afraid they'd come and sort us out.
Constable	Blowed if I see why they should – not if they really were getting all these bits as scrap off their dad's dustcart.

Fade to police station. The **Constable** *is interviewing the two* **Martin** *boys with their* **dad**.

Constable	I understand you're a dustman, Mr Martin.
Mr Martin	No, sir. Post office sorting clerk. Fifteen years now with the GPO.

Constable	I see. (*pause*) Right then, Leslie and Garry, let's have the truth about this Burner of Tony Rawlins.
Garry	It's like we already told you!
Leslie	Bought it off Stew and Frank for forty-two flippin' quid.
Constable	That's extremely cheap. You can pay hundreds of pounds for a new BMX.
Leslie	Ah, that's for the specials.
Constable	Come on now, you were getting a cannibal, and you knew it.
Mr Martin	(*confused*) How's that, officer?
Constable	Jargon, Mr Martin, for a bike with a resprayed frame and made up from parts cannibalised from several different bikes – all of them like as not stolen. (*pause*) Well, lads, was that why you went to buy one off Stewart Watson? Knowing he had a garage full of stolen BMX bikes?
Garry	We paid him all our dosh.
Constable	That's not what him and Frank Blair are saying.
Leslie	Forty-two quid!
Mr Martin	That's right, officer.
Constable	You gave them that money, did you, sir?
Mr Martin	Not one penny, no.
Leslie	(*proud*) We earned it all ourselves.
Constable	(*doubting*) Oh yes?
Mr Martin	See, that's how they been brought up. If they want anything, they work hard, they save up and they buy it with their own money. How else they ever going to learn to value things if they don't work for them like that?
Constable	I see, sir. (*pause*) Well now, lads, I have to tell you that Stewart and Frank deny selling you that Burner.
Garry	You what?
Constable	According to them, they assembled it from bits *you'd* brought to them.
Garry	Man, that's not true!
Constable	Furthermore, they're saying all the other parts and frames in their workshop – much of which is identifiable as stolen – were brought by you two to make up into cannibals.

Leslie	They're lying!
Constable	Certainly someone's lying, lad – you or them – or else all four of you.

Fade to next day. **Stewart** *and* **Frank** *are cornered by the two* **Martin** *boys on their way back from school.*

Garry	Hold it, you two scabs!
Frank	Get lost.
Garry	Not until we get some answers.
Frank	What about?
Leslie	Don't pretend you don't know.
Stewart	You better leave us alone!
Garry	Oh yeah? Or what?
Stewart	Tell the Law, that's what! Tell how you're threatening us!
Garry	(*pushing him*) Too right, we are, Stew-pot!
Stewart	Again.
Leslie	What d'you mean? We never did before.
Stewart	You did over that bike – that Burner you had.
Leslie	What about it?
Stewart	You know!
Leslie	Know what? All we know is you'd stolen it – nicked it off Tony Rawlins and then took all that dosh off us for it.
Frank	What dosh? You never give us no money!
Stewart	No!
Garry	*We did!*
Leslie	Stewart had it. Forty-two flippin' quid we paid him.
Stewart	You didn't! That's a lie!
Garry	(*pushing him again*) You're the liar! All that rap you told the Fuzz about us.
Stewart	I didn't – didn't!
Leslie	Look, the copper told us, Stewart – told us exactly what you said.
Stewart	(*quickly*) He was just stirring it – making it up as a trick. They always do!
Garry	(*another push*) You're going back to tell that copper the truth.

Stewart	Get lost!
Garry	You go, Stew-pot, or else!
Frank	Else what, Garry? What you going to do?
Garry	Sort you out, that's what!
Frank	Yeah? You and whose army?

*Fade, to that evening at the **Martin** home.*

Constable	Threatening them, Mr Martin. It seems they threatened to sort them out unless they changed their evidence.
Mr Martin	This isn't so, is it, boys?
Leslie	We were only after them to tell the truth, dad.
Mr Martin	Leslie, I *told* you . . .
Garry	But they're lying about us! Stirring it. What we supposed to do? Just say yeah, yeah, yeah?
Constable	You admit it then? Threatening Frank and Stewart after school? Also pushing them?
Garry	Man, it was just – just talk . . .
Constable	That's not what they're saying.
Leslie	Please, sir, Frank Blair's twice our size. How'd we ever sort him out? I mean, we'd be stupid to start getting rough with him.
Garry	Yeah, same as we'd be a couple of right wallies to go nicking bikes like they're making out. I mean, look how it is for black kids like us round here. The moment there's any trouble, we all know whose door the Law comes knocking on first.
Constable	Well you boys just stay well clear of those other two until the court case. Mr Martin, you'll be well advised to get them a solicitor for the court.
Mr Martin	Why? They aren't thieves.
Constable	Nevertheless, that's what they're charged with.
Mr Martin	Look, they paid for that bike.
Constable	Fine. But a lawyer'll tell it better than them. It won't cost you, sir, not with the Legal Aid scheme.
Mr Martin	It isn't the cost. The way I see it, lawyers are for people who lie. My two boys ain't liars.
Constable	Ah, but the magistrates won't know that.

Fade to court.

Magistrate   And you, Leslie – you're a BMX enthusiast? It's your hobby?

Leslie   Garry's the scrambles artist. Cup-holder. If he could get himself onto a proper race bike, he'd be way up to national standard.

Magistrate   My word. And what about you?

Leslie   (*proud*) See, I'm more into freestyle on the skate park. Bunny hops and that. I can manage a three-foot aerial on the quarter-pipe.

Magistrate   You make it sound almost like ballet dancing.

Leslie   Break-dancing, more like.

Prosecutor   It might interest the bench to know that the police have noticed a marked drop in juvenile crime since the BMX craze really caught on.

Magistrate   (*to* **Leslie**) And you say you saved up this money from your paper-round?

Leslie   Yes. When we'd got over forty saved, Stewart offered us this Superfox. Very pricy.

Prosecutor   Tell the magistrates about the negotiations then, Leslie.

Fade back to scene of the bike buying.

Stewart   There you are then really sneaky, isn't it. See these Mag wheels. Take a right bashing, they can.

Garry   Need to and all, the way Les whacks them around on the skate-park.

Leslie   How much you asking for it then?

Stewart   Eighty quid.

Garry   You *what?*

Stewart   Sixty-five, absolute minimum.

Garry   Flippin' heck!

Leslie   You're off your nut!

Stewart   A give-away at that price!

Garry   Yeah? And how much did *you* pay for it, Stew-pot?

Stewart   That'd be telling.

Garry   Too right!

Leslie   Picked it up cheap cos it needed a respray, did you?

Stewart	Look, if you can't afford it, take a look at this Burner I've got.
Garry	Call this a BMX?
Leslie	Load of old scrap, more like.
Stewart	If you haven't got the dosh for anything better . . .
Garry	How much then?
Stewart	What about sixty quid?
Leslie	Come on, we said our limit was forty.
Stewart	Okay, pay me forty down – now – and then another twenty by instalments. Like on hire purchase.
Garry	For an old Burner? No way!
Leslie	Forty's our limit.
Stewart	Forty-five.
Garry	Forty-one.
Stewart	Forty-two.
Garry	Okay, Les?
Leslie	Done!

Fade back into court.

Prosecutor	Garry, at that price, you *must* have suspected it was stolen.
Garry	No, sir!
Prosecutor	You were getting it for about a quarter of its real value and you didn't ask yourselves why?
Garry	We beat him down!
Prosecutor	(*doubtful*) If indeed you're telling the truth about paying them at all . . .
Garry	We did!
Prosecutor	Well that is for the magistrates to decide. (*to the bench*) Do your worships have any questions?
Magistrate	No thank you. You can sit down, Garry. Mr Martin, do you have anything you wish to say before we retire to consider our verdict?
Mr Martin	Only, sir, that my two boys have always been brought up totally straight. They'd no more have stolen that bike off this boy Tony than they'd lie to your worships about it under oath in court.

Magistrate	Thank you. (*pause*) Mrs Blair, do you want to say anything to us about Frank? No? How about you, Mrs Watson? Anything to say about Stewart?
Mrs Watson	Yes, I have. You see, Mr Martin's wrong about his youngsters. Those two have terrorised poor Stewart – bullied him and Frank into doing up those bikes for them. Whatever stealing went on was done by Garry and Leslie, not Stewart. He'd *never* have touched any of those bits and pieces if he'd known they were stolen. And another thing, I'm sure he never had a penny piece out of it from them or anyone else.
Magistrate	Thank you, Mrs Watson. We shall retire to consider the evidence.
	Pause. After the magistrates have left the court, **Garry** *and* **Leslie** *cross towards* **Tony Rawlins**.
Garry	Okay, Mr Detective, suppose you tell us where you got it.
Tony	Eh?
Garry	That Burner you reckon we stole off you – where'd you get it from?
Tony	Er . . .
Garry	*Where?*
Leslie	Take it easy, Garry. What you mouthing about?
Garry	Tony knows what I mean, don't you, Tony. Come on, admit it.
Leslie	Suppose you tell us then.
Garry	He bought it off Stew-pot Watson. Right, Tony?
Tony	Yeah . . . okay. (*Then, in a rush . . .*) And it was exactly the same way you just told the beaks: he offered me HP instalments and all that.
Garry	Right then, come over here and tell it to the law.
	Fade to later, still in court.
Prosecutor	Tell the magistrates why you didn't explain all this to them when you gave evidence earlier.
Tony	(*nervous*) Er, well, I suppose I was sort of, you know, scared to tell about it.

Prosecutor	Why?
Tony	You see, I went to Stewart for a BMX because I knew I'd get one on the cheap.
Prosecutor	Cheap because they're stolen?
Tony	(*mumbled*) Well, er, yes. Or cannibalised.
Prosecutor	Anything else to tell the magistrates?
Tony	(*pause*) I think Stewart was cheating Frank out of his share of the money.
Stewart	*No!*
Prosecutor	Be quiet, Stewart. Tell us, Tony.
Tony	You see, that day I bought the Burner, Stewart waited until Frank was out of the way before he agreed the price and took the money.
Stewart	No! You had it on approval. You were going to pay us later!
Tony	You had all sixty in cash – down!
Stewart	No! It's lies . . .
Prosecutor	Stewart, there have indeed been lies told here today. I think the magistrates now know by whom. Anything else, Tony?
Tony	He gave me a combination chain lock with the Burner. So I suppose that was how he was able to steal it back when I left it in the school bikeshed – because he'd have known the combination.
Prosecutor	Thank you, Tony, you've been very helpful.
Magistrate	Any other questions for Tony? (*pause*) No? Off and sit down again Tony, thank you. (*pause*) You four, stand up. (*pause*) Stewart John Watson, Frank Edward Blair, we find the case against you proved. Leslie and Garry, the charges against you are dismissed. Go and sit at the back with your parents. (*pause*) Now then, Stewart and Frank, we shall adjourn today's hearing so that reports can be prepared on you . . .

Fade to court three weeks later.

Magistrate	Stewart and Frank, we have now read the

background reports on you. We order that you must do twenty-four hours drill and training at an attendance centre. That means you willl lose your Saturday afternoons for the next twelve weeks. We also order that you return all the stolen BMX bikes and repay Leslie and Garry their money.

Questions for discussion and written work

□ □

Understanding the action

1 Before the truth was known at the end of the play, who did you think had been stealing the bikes?

2 When the policeman went to check the Martin boys' Burner at the BMX track, why do you think he suspected it was stolen?

3 How did Stewart Watson at first try to account for all the BMX parts in his garage and how did he then change his story?

Making up your mind

4 How would you react if you had a chance to buy something which you thought might be stolen? Talk about the battle going on inside you: knowing you could have something you wanted, but that it was dishonest.

5 Discuss how fair you think the police are in the way they deal (a) with children (b) with persistant villains (c) with motoring offenders (d) with black people.

6 How would you react if you found out that some boys at school were stealing regularly? Would it make any difference if they had stolen from you or from your best friend?

Ideas for writing

7 Write to an insurance company explaining that your bike has been stolen, giving details of the precautions you had taken to try and prevent it, what you then did to try and get it back, and also how much it will cost to replace.

8 Write a scene between three magistrates arguing about the best sentence for Stewart and Frank. One feels they should be fined, another favours probation, the third wants them to spend twelve Saturday afternoons at an attendance centre.

9 Write what you think the probation officer might have put in his background report on Stewart.

Drama work

10 Improvise a scene where your parents have decided not to give you any pocket money because they want you to learn to value money by earning it yourself.

11 Improvise a scene where a friend wants to start stealing BMX bikes and is trying to persuade you and other mates to go in with him.

12 Imagine a scene where you and some friends have been caught stealing and you are trying to explain to your parents why you did it.

Wagging It

Jamie Bilton, 12, is a mischievous terror to his teachers, his mum and his elder sister. His behaviour has got worse in the last few months since his dad left home.

Rob Bilton, 12, although led by his identical twin brother, is no less a cheeky handful.

Stephanie Bilton, 14, is podgy and plain and, like her twin brothers, a right scruff to look at. She, too, is missing her dad.

Mrs Bilton, depressed by the departure of her husband, now has the beaten-down, bewildered air of someone defeated by all the cares of the world.

Ms Cartwright, the social worker, is large, bulky and well meaning.

Also: classmates **Jane**, **Katherine**, **Tracy**, **Helen**, **Mark** and **Trevor**.

Also: **Lawyer**, **Magistrate**, **Teacher**, **Police constable**.

Fade in. The three **Bilton** *children are walking beside a busy road on their way to school.*

Steph	Come on or we'll miss assembly.
Jamie	Great, Steph.
Rob	Yeah, brill.
Steph	Get a move on or I'll thump the pair of you!
Jamie	But Steph . . . Hey look!
Rob	What's up?
Jamie	(*pointing*) It's dad!
Rob	Where?
Jamie	(*still pointing*) Look, driving that lorry. Hey, Dad! Dad!
Steph	Stop all the shouting.
Jamie	But it was dad!
Steph	Don't be stupid . . .

Jamie	Positive. Right, Rob?
Rob	(*unsure*) Well, yes.
Jamie	Come on then – quick . . .
Steph	Where?
Jamie	After him, of course.
Steph	Don't be stupid. He'll be miles away by now.
Jamie	He might stop.
Rob	Yes, there's that big lorry park. You know, the one near the arcade.
Jamie	Come on then!

Pause as they start along road.

Steph	Jamie, if this is another of your tricks . . .
Jamie	It was him, Steph. (*Suddenly he is fighting back tears, longing to find his dad.*) It was dad – *positive*.
Steph	Can't have been, though, can it – not if he's in Germany.
Rob	Those container lorries come from over there.
Jamie	Yeah! He could have driven it over!
Steph	No way.
Jamie	Why not, Steph?
Steph	Well, if he really was here, he'd have come home – come and seen us.
Jamie	(*near to tears*) It was him . . . *really* . . .
Steph	(*realising Jamie is sincere*) Okay then, okay. (*pause*) Anyway, let's get to school.
Rob	No!
Steph	Look, we promised mum!
Jamie	Yeah, but, Steph . . .
Steph	(*persisting*) You know what'll happen to her if we keep on wagging it. You know what old Cartwright told us.
Jamie	I hate her!
Rob	Right. (*Puts on Star Wars voice.*) Darth Veda – exterminate!
Jamie	Come on, Rob, I'll zap you.
Rob	No chance. Pow! You're dead!
Steph	Not those flippin' Space Invaders – not again!

Jamie	Yes!
Rob	10p Steph. Come on!
Steph	Ain't got it.
Jamie	Have! In here. (*He snatches her school-bag.*)
Steph	Give that back!
Jamie	(*tosses purse from her bag*) Catch, Rob . . .
Steph	Mum gave me that for the groceries.
Jamie	We'll get the stuff for you, don't worry.
Rob	(*giggling*) Yes. Easy!
Steph	You two'll get yourselves locked up and all.

Fade to **Bilton** *home that afternoon.*

Steph	Hi, mum. (*pause*) Mum?
Mrs Bilton	You're back then.
Steph	(*brightly*) Got you the groceries – well, mostly.
Mrs Bilton	Stephanie . . .
Steph	(*quickly*) I'll give the place a clear-up. It's a right old mess in here. Where you been all day?
Mrs Bilton	Where've *you* been, my girl?
Jamie	Hey, mum, anything to eat?
Rob	Yeah, I'm starving.
Steph	You just leave those biscuits, Rob!
Rob	But . . .
Steph	Tell him, mum.
Mrs Bilton	(*losing patience*) Listen to me . . . LISTEN! (*startled pause*) Why'd you do it, eh? Truanting again.
Steph	Mum . . .
Mrs Bilton	(*persisting*) It's no good pretending. I had the man round again from the school. (*pause*) They'll have me back in court, you know. (*pause*) Why'd you do it, eh?
Jamie	See, mum, we were almost at school when there was this big lorry and . . .
Steph	(*interrupting him*) Forget it, Jamie.
Jamie	But . . .
Steph	(*quickly to her mother*) Sorry mum. Honest.
Mrs Bilton	(*distressed*) Doctor keeps on at me to stop

worrying. Some hope of that, the way you lot carry on.

Fade to school playground the next morning.

Jane	Hey, look who's here!
Katherine	(*jeering*) What an honour!
Tracy	Come slumming it today, Stephanie?
Steph	Shove off, you lot!
Helen	Didn't bother to wash her hair though, did she.
Tracy	(*giggles*) Greasy hair's all the rage, silly.
	All four girls laugh mockingly.
Jane	Right, Trace – to go with the flaired collar.
Katherine	Where'd your mum get it, Stephanie? Oxfam?
Tracy	How could she? Her mum's never out of the pub.
	Again they all screech with laughter.
Steph	Shut it, Tracy – that's a rotten thing to say!
Katherine	(*mocking*) Yes, Tracy, 'rotten'.
Jamie	(*pushing in*) Leave her alone!
Jane	Wow – watch out – Superman's here!
Helen	(*giggling*) Flipping 'eck! Where's Robin?
Jamie	Come on, Steph.
Jane	Not so fast . . .
Jamie	Stop pushing us, Jane!
Steph	It's okay, Jamie, just ignore them.
Katherine	Can't ignore you lot, can we! All stink of that tip you live in!
Rob	(*pushing in*) It ain't a tip!
Katherine	Hey, titch, watch who you're shoving!
Jane	Taking on the heavies, are you?
Rob	Ouch! (*He half falls from a push.*)
Steph	(*pushing to his defence*) Hateful pigs!
Katherine	(*swinging Steph by an arm*) One-parent wonders!
Jane	(*shoving at the twins*) Get lost, go on!
Helen	(*also attacking*) Run, run, run!
	*The three **Biltons** run from the playground.*
Katherine	(*calling after them*) School can do without stink freaks like you lot!

Fade to later in High Street.

Steph   Jamie, where've you been?

Jamie   (*giggles*) 'Shopping.'

Steph   Nicking, more like. Where's Rob?

Jamie   Said he'd meet us down the arcade.

Steph   I told the pair of you . . .

Jamie   (*interrupting*) Steph, we can't go back to school – not with all this stuff.

Steph   Give it here, then. (*taking it*) Biscuits . . . cheese snacks . . . crisps . . . you're blooming daft to take so much.

Jamie   It's dead easy.

Steph   Oh, sure – until you get caught again.

Rob   (*breathless as he joins them*) Caught?

Jamie   It's okay. What you got then?

Rob   (*mutter*) Nothing.

Jamie   What?

Rob   Man saw me. He chased me out the shop.

Jamie   Phew!

Steph   Oh, Robbie . . .

Rob   (*brightly*) Give us a go on the machines then.

Jamie   Yes! Share it out, Steph.

Steph   50p each and no more.

Rob   Hey. Meanie!

Jamie   All that stuff I just got you!

Constable   (*abrupt as he comes up*) What stuff, lad? (*heavy pause*) Open up, Stephanie. Let's see what's in the bag. (*another pause*) Terrible how you always go for the junk-food. (*He points along the street.*) Come along then, the three of you – off down the station.

Jamie   (*miserably*) What'll happen?

Constable   Depends. You could be in court this time.

Both twins promptly start wailing.

Constable   (*continued*) Hush up that row, you two. (*pause*) Look, if you come clean and help return all this stuff to the shop you may get away with another caution from the Inspector.

Fade to **Bilton** *home that afternoon.*

Mrs Cartwright Hello children.

Steph What you doing here?

Mrs Bilton (*warningly*) Steph . . .

Steph (*to* **Mrs Cartwright**) What you been saying to mum?

Mrs Cartwright Pardon, Stephanie?

Mrs Bilton Nothing, Steph, it's okay.

Steph Then why've you been crying, eh?

Mrs Bilton (*not wanting a fuss*) I told you, dear, it's nothing.

Mrs Cartwright There's tea in the pot, children – mugs on the drainer.

Rob Anything to eat?

Mrs Cartwright Biscuits – there you are.

Jamie (*to* **Rob**) Hey, give 'em over!

Steph (*to the social worker*) Is it about all that with the police?

Mrs Cartwright Partly, yes. Next time they'll prosecute you in court and . . .

Steph (*curt*) Won't be no next time.

Rob No!

Mrs Cartwright (*disbelieving*) Like always, eh.

Jamie There won't.

Mrs Cartwright As you know, the Social Services have been trying to help your mother, what with your father being away for so long.

Steph He's on a job in Germany.

Mrs Cartwright (*hiding the truth*) Ah – well now – be that as it may, it has caused a lot of problems.

Steph (*quickly*) We can manage.

Mrs Cartwright On the contrary, Stephanie, it's obvious you can't.

Steph (*sharp*) How'd you mean?

Mrs Cartwright Quite apart from the police, there's been all this truanting.

Steph That's all done with.

Rob Yeah.

Mrs Cartwright (*dismissive*) Again, like always.

Steph This time it's proper.

Jamie Yeah!

Mrs Cartwright	I'm sorry, children, but it's obvious you're totally beyond the control of your mother.
Jamie	(*interrupting*) We're *not!*
Mrs Cartwright	You've left us no alternative but to apply to the magistrates for a Care Order.
Jamie	*Why?*
Rob	What for?
Steph	To take us away?
Jamie	You *can't!*
Rob	(*shrill*) Tell her, mum! Tell her no!

Fade to the next day on the way to school.

Jamie	I hate her.
Rob	Old dough-bag!
Steph	It isn't *her* fault.
Jamie	It *is*.
Rob	Darth Veda. (*Puts on 'Star Wars' voice.*) Exterminate!
Jamie	They can't do it.
Steph	They can.
Jamie	Okay then, if they do, we'll run away!
Rob	What?
Jamie	If they stick us in one of them places, we'll push off.
Steph	Stupid wallie.
Jamie	I'm not! They're like prisons, them places.
Steph	Foster homes, that's where they'll shove us.
Rob	How'd you know?
Steph	Because I do.
Jamie	Mum won't let 'em.
Steph	Ain't nothing she can do.
Jamie	Foster homes means they'd split us up!
Rob	(*alarmed*) Why?
Jamie	Bound to!
Rob	(*starting to wail*) No . . .
Steph	(*soothing him*) It's okay, Robbie love, they won't.
Jamie	How'd you know that?
Steph	Because I won't let 'em, that's how.

| Rob | You sure, Steph? |
| **Steph** | Yes . . . on condition you two behave yourselves from now on. Okay? No more trouble! |

Fade to classroom later that day.

Teacher	Be quiet 1B! Quieten down! James Bilton, I saw that. You flicked that pellet. Stand up, please. (**James** *decides to pretend that he is his identical twin,* **Rob**.)
James	You said James, Miss. I'm Rob.
Teacher	Nonsense.
James	Honest. I am!
Teacher	You've brought yourselves to my attention often enough, James, for me to know which is which.
Rob	No, Miss, *I'm* James.
Trevor	He is, Miss.
Mark	That's right, Miss.
Teacher	Be quiet. (*pause*) Both Biltons, stand up. (*They do so.*) Both Biltons will stay in for detention tomorrow after school.
Jamie	(*outraged*) Hey!
Rob	That's not fair!
Jamie	Can't punish him because of me!
Teacher	I'm punishing both of you for lying.
Rob	We're not lying!
Jamie	*No!* (*He turns to* **Rob**) Come on! She's no right saying that. We're not staying here . . .
Teacher	(*abrupt*) Sit down! Both of you!
Jamie	No! We're leaving. (*Beckons to* **Rob** *and in his excitement, he forgets to pretend.*) Come on, Rob – er. I mean, Jamie!

The entire class errupt with laughter – to the silent relief of the teacher.

Fade to **Bilton** *home that afternoon.*

| **Steph** | Hi, mum. |

Mrs Bilton	All right at school today, was it?
Steph	(*awkward*) Well . . . yeah . . .
Mrs Bilton	(*sighs*) Oh, Steph . . .
Steph	See, they got into a bit of aggro with the geography teacher.
Mrs Bilton	(*crushed*) Oh lord . . . What's wrong with them, Steph? Why'd they have to play up all the time?
Steph	It's just . . .
Mrs Bilton	What?
Steph	Well, it's much worse since Dad went.
	Long pause.
Steph	(*continued*) Mum, will he be there?
Mrs Bilton	What?
Steph	Dad – will he be at the court?
Mrs Bilton	(*sharp*) What you think? What you expect?

Fade to juvenile court the next day.

Mrs Cartwright	Your worships, Mrs Bilton was not taken back to court over the truanting because by then the Social Services were aware of her health problems; also we had found out about the husband.
Magistrate	Found out?
Mrs Cartwright	Previously Mrs Bilton had pretended he was working over in Germany. She had concealed the fact of his deserting the family.
Jamie	(*startled*) You what?
Rob	(*distressed*) Mum?
Mrs Cartwright	(*to magistrate*) We've now found out he's living with a family down south.
Rob	(*more distressed*) Mum?
Magistrate	It seems the children were also under the impression he was in Germany.
Mrs Cartwright	Yes, your worship.
Lawyer	Ironically, sir, the reason they give for truanting is that they've been searching for their father.
Jamie	We were!
Magistrate	But why, James, if you thought he was abroad?

Jamie	We've *seen* him.
Rob	Yes!
Jamie	Seen him driving this big truck!
Magistrate	Mrs Cartwright, does Mr Bilton in fact work as a driver?
Mrs Cartwright	Not officially, sir. For the last few months, he's been drawing unemployment benefit down in London.
Magistrate	I see.
Lawyer	Are you sure you're not making all this up?
Steph	All what?
Lawyer	Aren't you inventing all this about seeing your father?
Steph	Why should we?
Lawyer	As an excuse perhaps, for all the truanting? (*pause*) We heard how, when you do get to school, all three of you are persistantly at the centre of trouble. Noisy and disruptive in class, frequently involved in playground fights.
Jamie	Because they're always ragging us, that's why.
Rob	Ain't fair!
Jamie	Calling us dirty scruffs and that.
Rob	Oxfam freaks . . .
Jamie	One-parent wonders . . .
Steph	Ain't very nice, you know. Anyone'd start wagging it for that.
Magistrate	Wagging what?
Lawyer	Playground slang, sir, for truanting. Also known as bunking it and nicking off.
Magistrate	Why didn't your mother go and complain about all this ragging at school?
Steph	Didn't tell her.
Magistrate	Whyever not?
Steph	She had worries of her own, didn't she.
Lawyer	Indeed, she had. Which is why the Social Services are applying for this order today. So that your mother can have a complete break and get on top of her worries.
Steph	We can manage.

Lawyer	But can *she?*
Steph	We're a family.
Jamie	**Yes!**
Steph	We've got to stick together.
Rob	Tell him, Mum!
Lawyer	Well, Mrs Bilton? Would you be happy about the children going into care for a while?
Mrs Bilton	(*pause*) No.
Lawyer	Why not?
Mrs Bilton	Well, you heard them: they don't want it. We can manage as we are.
Lawyer	Oh? According to Mrs Cartwright, things have slipped into a pretty hopeless mess. No money, no benefits, bills unpaid, the children neglected, running wild and stealing . . .
Mrs Bilton	I – I've been unwell.
Lawyer	And unlikely fully to recover, Mrs Bilton, because what you in fact need is a total rest.
Mrs Bilton	(*distressed*) Need, need . . . They need me, that's all I know.
Lawyer	But, Mrs Bilton . . .
Mrs Bilton	(*persisting*) They've lost their dad. It can't be right they should have to lose me and all.
Lawyer	But you know it won't be for very long.
Mrs Bilton	Sometime's a day is too long – long as forever. (*pause*)

Fade to later in court.

Magistrate	If the children were fostered, would all three be together?
Mrs Cartwright	Yes, sir, I'm happy to say so. A most caring family.
Magistrate	Thank you. (*to the children*) Stephanie, James, Robert, we have decided to make a care order. (*The children gasp in distress.*)
Magistrate	(*continued*) The length of time you're away will depend on you. If you try hard, improve your school attendance and behaviour, then it won't be for very long.

Questions for discussion and written work

□□□

Understanding the action

1   Before the magistrates announced their decision at the end of the play, what outcome did you expect?

2   What did the Bilton children do to make Mrs Cartwright say they were beyond their mother's control?

3   What was it that had made Mrs Bilton so ill she had to go to the doctor?

Making up your mind

4   How would you go about helping the Bilton family? Do you think the decision to take the three children away from their mother for a while was the right one? Explain you opinion.

5   How would you react if you thought your parents were splitting up? Would you talk about it to anyone – such as, say, your parents, your brother or sister, your grandparents, your closest friend, your teacher or even a total stranger?

6   Talk about the police decision to give the Bilton children yet another caution instead of sending them to court charged with shoplifting. Do you think a caution equals a let-off? Do you think children from broken homes deserve softer treatment than others?

Ideas for writing

7   Write a letter to a close friend telling him or her that your parents are splitting up and how you feel about it.

8   Write a newspaper article about an outbreak of truanting among teenagers, and the steps being taken by the school, the council and the courts to try and reduce it.

9   Imagine you are a social worker writing a report on the behaviour of the Bilton children and the state of their mother.

Drama work

10   Improvise a group scene where some pupils try to talk others out of truanting and shoplifting in order to play the machines down at the local arcade.

11   Improvise a scene where several children start to rag a classmate but then have a change of heart when they see the unhappiness it is causing the child. They try to make it up to their victim; but he or she distrusts them and ends up telling the teacher.

12   Improvise a scene where children come home and tell their mother they're in trouble again. She reacts by breaking down and telling them she can't cope.